Fascism

Richard Tames

HODDER
Wayland

Limerick
County Library

an imprint of Hodder Children's Books

Copyright © Hodder Wayland 2000

Published in Great Britain in 2000 by Hodder Wayland, a division of Hodder Children's Books.

This paperback edition published in 2003.

This book was prepared for Hodder Wayland by Ruth Nason.

Series design: Simon Borrough

The right of Richard Tames to be identified as the author of this work has been asserted by him in accordance with the Copyright, Designs and Patents Act 1988.

A catalogue record for this book is available from the British Library.

ISBN 0 7502 4608 1

Printed in Italy

Hodder Children's Books
A division of Hodder Headline Limited
338 Euston Road, London NW1 3BH

Acknowledgements
The author and publishers thank the following for permission to reproduce photographs: Camera Press: pages 5, 9, 23, 32, 48, 52, 57; Hulton Getty: pages 4, 6, 11, 12, 13, 17, 20, 24, 26b, 29, 30, 31, 35, 36, 38, 40, 46, 47; Popperfoto: pages 15, 16, 18, 19, 21, 26t, 27, 28, 37, 43, 44, 45, 56, 58. The maps were drawn by Carole Binding.

Contents

What is Fascism?

Fascism is easier to recognize than define. Nowadays, 'fascist!' tends to be used vaguely for anyone with violent, vicious political views. Historically, fascism was a type of political movement which aimed to unite a country's people into a disciplined force under an all-powerful leader. This leader would overcome all conflicts and failures, creating a glorious future – a nation reborn.

Fascism appealed to ex-servicemen, many of whom, failing to find work, became poor, embittered drifters. They were used to violence. Many missed army comradeship and a disciplined routine. Fascist movements offered what they needed: comrades, uniforms, orders, personal pride and a patriotic purpose.

Forgotten heroes (below left): defeated or victorious, many ex-servicemen in the 1920s were reduced to street-hawking, one step up from begging outright.

When did fascism emerge?

Fascist movements were born out of the First World War (1914-18), which tore Europe apart. Over 8,500,000 men were killed and over 21,000,000 wounded, gassed or otherwise injured. The victors, Britain and France, faced war debts, the cost of caring for the disabled and orphaned, and the challenge of getting millions out of armies and into work. It was far worse for defeated countries. The empires of Russia, Germany and Austria-Hungary all broke up, losing their monarchs and frontiers. Russia collapsed into civil war as communists seized power. Germany and Hungary faced communist uprisings. Throughout much of Europe, therefore, peace did not bring security or prosperity but fighting on the streets, riots, refugees, unemployment and fear of general chaos. This was an ideal breeding-ground for men and movements claiming to know how to restore order and national pride and lead their country to a brighter future.

The word 'fascist' comes from the name of the movement founded in Italy by Benito Mussolini: the *Fascio di Combattimenti* (League of Veterans). It also comes from the symbol that Mussolini took for the movement: the fasces, a bundle of wooden rods, bound with a red thong, with an axe-head sticking out. In ancient Rome the fasces had been carried before the magistrates, as a symbol of their authority. For Mussolini and his followers, the axe stood for power over life and death, and the rods for strength in unity.

The fascist movements which arose in different countries are all distinct from each other, but usually share some common features:

Authority. Power flows down from the leader, not up from the people.
Populism. Propaganda and organization are used to stir up ordinary people to become energetic but obedient followers.
Nativism. The traditions and heritage of the nation are held superior to all others.
Violence. This is evidence of strength, to be used against political enemies.
Anti-communism. Communism claims that the material world is the only reality. It denies religion and stresses class as the basis of identity and an international order without nations. Fascism regards nations as the basis of identity and international order, and claims a spiritual dimension of duty, loyalty, honour, courage and self-sacrifice. Anti-communism has often caused fascism and the Roman Catholic Church to become allies.

Mussolini the Prophet

Benito Mussolini commented on Hitler coming to power in 1933:

'Fascism is a religion; the 20th century will be known in history as the century of Fascism.'

Right, right: dictators in step towards destiny. Benito Mussolini (left) and Adolf Hitler offered to restore their countries to greatness.

Fascist movements and fascist states

There have been many fascist movements, but only two managed to turn a major country into a fascist state: Italy under Benito Mussolini (1922-43) and Germany under Adolf Hitler (1933-45).

A fascist state is a revolutionary dictatorship which smashes any individuals or institutions opposing its vision of national rebirth. Some countries, such as Spain, looked like fascist states – but they did so basically to seek stability, not revolution. They worked with existing powerful groups (armed forces, Church, government officials, large landowners and big business), rather than stirring up ordinary people to challenge the power of these groups and create a new kind of society. Fascist movements in the democracies of Western Europe have sometimes been a noisy nuisance but never seriously threatened to take over.

Catching them young: Hitler Youth drummers at the 1935 Nuremberg Rally.

Fascism and democracy

Fascists argue that, under the right leader, a nation can become perfect and therefore it is right to use any means necessary to achieve this. By contrast, democracy is based on the idea that people have differing interests and beliefs and no person or group is always right about everything. Democratic politics is not about forcing people in a single direction but about persuading them to resolve conflicts by compromise and to get along together. In a democracy, political decisions are made by talking. Democracy relies on parliaments (from the French 'parler' – to talk) to debate all sides of an argument before a decision is made. Parliaments focus wider discussions among political parties, trade unions, churches, community groups and the mass media.

Decision-making in a democracy is often slow, confusing and frustrating. Few get exactly what they want and most put up with things with which they do not entirely agree. One appeal of fascism was that it avoided the messy business of democratic debate. Fascists argued that democratic compromises betrayed one's beliefs. Fascist politics was about giving orders, not making deals. Fascism claimed to be faster and more efficient. Obey the leader and everything will be fine. Common slogans in Fascist Italy were 'Mussolini is always right!' and 'Believe! Obey! Fight!'

Mussolini and Hitler claimed dictatorship was right because democracy had failed, leaving their countries in crisis. They also deliberately created crises so that their powers would continue to seem necessary. And they managed politics so that their countries looked like democracies – except that their parliaments had no real powers, the mass media no real freedom and the only organizations allowed to exist were those they controlled.

The power of the nation

As a journalist Mussolini was trained to think in headlines. As *Duce* he posed as a philosopher of high ideals:

'For us the nation is not just territory, but something spiritual. There are States which have had immense territories and which have left no trace in human history ... A nation is great when it translates into reality the force of its spirit.'

Totalitarianism

Fascism and communism are both totalitarian systems, in which the state is supreme over everyone and everything. Totalitarianism aims at total control. Even leisure is considered a political matter. The films people watch, the books they read and the sports they play are all to serve political ends. Mussolini banned jazz and Hitler had books by Jews and communists burned. A novel by George Orwell, *Nineteen Eighty-Four*, published in 1949, describes life in a totalitarian state, ruled by 'Big Brother' and the 'Thought Police', where children spy on their parents and everyone joins in organized hate sessions against traitors.

Fascism and communism

After 1918, fascism rivalled communism as the main challenge to democracy. On the surface, no two systems could be more different. Fascists fought communists on the streets and the battlefield. Communism claimed to be creating a society of equals, whereas fascism declared that some individuals and races were unalterably superior. Communists believed the state should control all businesses. Fascists allowed private businesses to make big profits, as long as they supplied the state's needs.

Fascism and communism both appealed to people impatient with democracy, who thought their country had gone soft and selfish and needed more discipline and direction. Both fascism and communism were revolutionary movements, aiming to break with the past and create a new society. Anyone who disagreed with this noble aim was a traitor to be beaten, imprisoned or killed.

Leaders and laws

Fascist and communist states made constant use of propaganda, posters, slogans, uniforms, rallies, parades and festivals to play on the pride, loyalties, fears and hatreds of their followers. Emotion, not reasoning, was the key to the politics linking leader and led.

Both fascist and communist states built 'personality cults'. The leader was presented to the people as a genius – a deep thinker and bold man of action, a brilliant commander of armies and a loving father to the nation, the perfect model of strength, wisdom, courage and compassion. The leader had the right to demand total trust and obedience because he knew where History was heading and how to take his people towards their glorious destiny.

The far right Freedom Party, led by Jörg Haider, an SS officer's son, joined an Austrian coalition government in 2000. This prompted Europe-wide demonstrations, calling that fascism should never be allowed again.

Mussolini and Hitler were actually cunning and cruel, rather than clever and caring. Because they had almost unlimited power, their particular personalities mattered very much. The fact that Hitler had a fanatical hatred of Jews and thought gypsies, homosexuals and the deformed or mentally disabled were worthless as human beings condemned over six million people to slavery and death.

Both fascism and communism ignored the rule of law in favour of the leader's orders. In a democracy, all government officials, police, armed forces and judges should follow rules laid down by lawmakers in parliament and deal with everyone equally. In totalitarian states, the law is just another tool to control people. Police arrest political opponents ('enemies'), and judges obediently send them to prison. Judges applying the law against the leader's wishes are soon dismissed. Secret police often arrest people to be tortured or murdered without even bothering to pretend that a law has been broken.

The end of fascism?

The fascist states and their followers emerged after the First World War and were destroyed in the Second, but fascist movements continue to re-invent themselves, especially where a country is in crisis – or can be made to look like it. The fascism that was is a warning from history of the fascism that might be again.

Classic Fascism Italy 1922-43

Unity and Empire

Between 1859 and 1871 Italy was unified by wars which ended Austro-Hungarian rule over the north of the country and put the rest under the king of Piedmont Sardinia, Victor Emmanuel II. But united Italy remained backward, producing less steel than even little Belgium. The south, Sicily and Sardinia remained wretchedly poor. In 1900, when Victor Emmanuel III became king, half the Italian population was still illiterate. Politics was cursed by corruption and short-lived, unstable governments. Between 1880 and 1914 over 8,000,000 Italians emigrated for a better life in the USA and Argentina.

0   200   400 Km

0   125   250 Miles

SWITZER-LAND
AUSTRIA
Tyrol
Trentino Trieste
Milan
Fiume
Bologna
YUGOSLAVIA
Istria
Dalmatian Coast
Florence
CORSICA
ITALY
Rome
GREECE
ALBANIA
Naples
SARDINIA
CORFU
TURKEY
SICILY
CRETE
NORTH AFRICA
Italian gains, 1919-20

ITALY
TURKEY
800 Km
500 Miles
Mediterranean Sea
ALGERIA
LIBYA
EGYPT
SAUDI ARABIA
ERITREA
ETHIOPIA
ITALIAN SOMALILAND

Italy imitated other European powers by conquering an overseas empire, starting with Eritrea and part of Somalia. Its invasion of Ethiopia ended in humiliating defeat at Adowa (1896). In 1911-12 Italy took Libya and the Dodecanese Islands from Ottoman Turkey.

The green shading shows Italy's empire by the time Mussolini came to power. He would add the port of Fiume, in 1924, and Ethiopia, in 1935-36.

War

Italy remained neutral in 1914 but joined the Allies in 1915, in return for promised territories from Austria-Hungary. Italy launched eleven attacks along its mountainous northeast frontier, gaining just seven miles. In October 1917, the Austrians, reinforced by Germans, counter-attacked at Caporetto and pushed the Italians back many miles, taking 250,000 prisoners. Italian victory at Vittorio Veneto in 1918 salvaged some national pride, but Italy ended the war with 600,000 dead and little to show for it. South Tyrol, Trentino and Trieste became Italian, but the port of Fiume and the Dalmatian coast did not.

What did we fight for? The endurance of Italy's troops in the First World War brought little reward.

Past Against Future

When the First World War broke out, the poet Filippo Marinetti (1876-1944) predicted that it would give Italy the chance to break with the past:

'The War will sweep from power all [Italy's] foes: diplomats, professors ... archaeologists ... Greek, Latin, history ... museums, libraries, the tourist industry. The War will promote gymnastics, sport, practical schools of agriculture, business and industry. The War will renew Italy, enrich her with men of action, force her to live no longer off the past, off ruins and the mild climate, but off her own national forces.'

Marinetti became and remained a strong supporter of fascism.

Working days lost in strikes	
1918 –	912,000
1919 –	22,325,000
1920 –	30,569,000
1921 –	8,180,000
1922 –	6,917,000
1923 –	296,000

Italy on the brink

Between 1919 and 1921 Italy seemed to slide towards civil war. War debts damaged national finances. Angry peasants demanded land reform. Rioters demanded cheaper bread. Trade union membership grew from 250,000 in 1918 to 2,300,000 in 1920. In Milan, Bologna and Florence, 500,000 workers seized control of factories. Politicians, divided between liberals, socialists and Catholics, seemed powerless to govern firmly. In 1921 a socialist group split off to form an Italian communist party. It was more prepared than the socialists to plan for violent revolution.

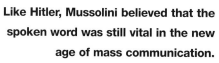

Like Hitler, Mussolini believed that the spoken word was still vital in the new age of mass communication.

Benito Mussolini (1883-1945) The making of a dictator

Mussolini's father, a blacksmith and socialist town councillor, named his son after a Mexican revolutionary, Benito Juarez. As a boy, Benito Mussolini proved bright but violent. He was expelled from school five times, twice for stabbing fellow pupils. By age 30 he had been a teacher, labourer, agitator, army deserter, journalist, union organizer, prisoner and editor of the Socialist Party newspaper *Avanti!* (*Forwards!*). Supporting Italian involvement in the First World War cost him that job, but he soon became editor of *Il Popolo d'Italia* (*The People of Italy*), financed by a pro-war publisher. Conscripted in 1915, he became a corporal until wounded in an accident and invalided out in 1917.

Gabriele d'Annunzio
A man of action

Famous as a poet from the age of 16, d'Annunzio (1863-1938) fought in the First World War, losing an eye in combat and winning an award for bravery. A daring air raid over Vienna in 1918 made him a national hero. In 1919, while Italy and Yugoslavia quarrelled over the former Austro-Hungarian port of Fiume, d'Annunzio seized it with a band of war veterans and ruled it as a dictator until an Italian battleship, enforcing a treaty that Fiume should be independent, bombarded them out. Although d'Annunzio had failed, he was admired for acting boldly while others talked. He became a strong supporter of fascism, but preferred writing to active politics. Mussolini made Fiume Italian in 1924 and gave d'Annunzio many honours.

Respect for a hero: Mussolini appears to listen attentively to Gabriele d'Annunzio.

A revolution from the trenches?

As editor of *Il Popolo d'Italia*, in December 1917, Mussolini predicted:

'A new aristocracy is emerging ... The disabled servicemen of today are the vanguard of the great army who will return tomorrow. They are the thousands who await millions of demobilized soldiers. This enormous mass ... is bound to shake up society. The brutal and bloody apprenticeship of the trenches will mean ... more courage, more faith, more strength. The old parties, the old men ... will be swept aside ...'

The first fascists

Mussolini founded the first *Fascio di Combattimenti* (League of Veterans) in Milan on 13 March 1919. Its 200 members were the pioneers of a movement which attracted new members through rallies at which Mussolini proved himself a superb mob orator. His facts were often wrong, his ideas a muddle, and his attacks on opponents unfair, but he looked tough and sounded tougher. Direct action also encouraged recruits. On 15 April, fascists gathered a mob to attack a socialist demonstration in Milan and smash up the offices of the Socialist Party newspaper *Avanti!*

Mussolini's aims were large but vague: a fair deal for war veterans; Fiume, Dalmatia and an overseas empire for Italy; and violent opposition to communists. Later he added reforms to help poor peasants. His main followers were ex-soldiers, disgusted with the war's outcome. They were joined by students and intellectuals, hopeful for a brighter future which would fulfil the original promise of an Italy united for greatness. The early fascists were drawn together less by specific plans than by their general mood – '*Me no frego*' ('I don't care what anyone thinks ...').

In 1921, Mussolini, claiming (but not necessarily having) 300,000 supporters, formed a National Fascist Party and was elected to the Chamber of Deputies, the lower house of Italy's parliament. Many businessmen and landowners, frightened of trade union and peasant demands, welcomed the Fascists as a weapon against communists and socialists. When landless labourers invaded large estates, landowners loaned lorries to Fascist squads so that they could bring men from the cities to throw the labourers out. In May 1922, Fascists took over the local government of Bologna, in August of Milan.

The Blackshirts

Black shirts were worn by the *Arditi*, Italy's crack assault troops of the First World War. As Mussolini's earliest followers included many former Arditi, the black shirt was a natural uniform. Uniforms made Fascist squads look disciplined and identified them from enemies in street-fighting. Distinctive shirts – in Germany brown, in Britain black, in Ireland blue – became a feature of other fascist movements.

Black-shirted *squadristi* were the core members and most visible aspect of Italy's Fascist movement in its early days. In 1923, after Mussolini came to power, Fascist squads became part of a new Voluntary Militia for National Security, paid for out of taxes. This brought them under greater discipline and enabled Mussolini to reward followers with jobs in the militia's ranks.

From democracy to dictatorship

In October 1922, Fascist groups began taking over railway stations, post offices, telephone exchanges and other public buildings. They claimed that, if the country was sliding into a chaos of riots and strikes, they would patriotically keep communications going. When socialist leaders announced a general strike, Mussolini demanded that the government stop it – or the Fascists would march on Rome and take over themselves. In fear of general disorder, or even civil war, Victor Emmanuel III, acting as guardian of the constitution, invited Mussolini to become prime minister – the youngest in Italy's history. So, technically, Mussolini came to power legally, but this was obscured by the 'March on Rome'. Squads converged on the capital as though seizing power by force, like true revolutionaries. Mussolini arrived undramatically by train, but insisted on a 'victory parade' through the city.

At first, Mussolini governed at the head of a coalition of parties and few of his ministers were Fascists. In November, the king and parliament gave Mussolini powers of dictatorship for one year. He improved his image by giving up drinking and smoking, and travelled around being photographed for the newspapers, looking like a serious, hard-working leader.

Gateway to the future: Fascisti march through Rome's Porto del Popolo, 28 October 1922.

On 1 June 1924, socialist leader Giacomo Matteotti spoke out against Fascists for beating up opponents in elections. The 1924 elections were undoubtedly fixed by Fascist bullying and corruption, but they were enough to secure Mussolini in power. After that, elections became irrelevant. The last words of Matteotti's speech were, 'And now get ready for my funeral.' On 10 June, he was kidnapped by Fascist bullies. His body was found months later. In protest, the opposition parties walked out of parliament. Mussolini suspended it.

Building a dictatorship

In 1925 Mussolini took the title of *Il Duce* (the Leader). Strikes were banned – a popular move with most non-unionists. Only state-controlled unions and newspapers were allowed. Crime reports were banned. So were beauty contests. Police powers of arrest were increased. Mafia leaders and communists were imprisoned. In 1926 the Fascists became the only legal political party.

Charming Churchill

British politician Winston Churchill wrote in *The Times* in 1927:

'I could not help being charmed ... by Signor Mussolini's gentle and simple bearing and by his calm detached poise in spite of so many burdens and dangers.'

Disciplined young people marching in uniform symbolized the hope of national unity that fascism promised.

The true uses of leisure

Achille Starace (1889-1945), director of the National Leisure System, explained the purpose of some of its activities for youth:

'to know the true face of the Fatherland by travelling along its roads ... To make them expert at swimming and climbing, and in the skills which may be necessary in a future war! To loosen their muscles in joyful and simple sporting contests ...'

Only party members were allowed to hold government jobs or become judges. Even teachers were made to wear Fascist uniforms. Parliament was replaced by a complicated but powerless Chamber of Corporations, which was supposed to represent all the nation's differing groups – business, workers, farmers, students, officials and so on.

Compared to most dictatorships, Italian Fascism was not particularly brutal. Beatings were routine enough, but, over the whole period of Fascist power, only 4,000 political opponents were imprisoned and ten

Leading from the front: Achille Starace, secretary general of the Fascist Party, leaps through a burning hoop at a physical fitness contest, arranged by order of Mussolini, in Rome, July 1938.

Fascist organizations

Mussolini's ambition to create a strong Italy required a large army. So, to encourage more births and healthier babies, a National Agency for Maternity and Infancy was founded. For the same reason, bachelors were taxed to encourage them to marry, and women were banned from government jobs.

From 1925, a National Leisure System (*Opera nazionale dopolavoro*) promoted healthy recreation such as climbing and swimming. To encourage loyalty to *Il Duce* and party, there were nationwide youth movements, the *Balilla* for boys aged 8-14 and the *Avanguardisti* for teenagers 15-17.

executed. Extreme measures were justified by the need to protect Mussolini, who survived four assassination attempts. Although Mussolini allowed the king no real power, he treated him with outward respect and never tried to abolish the monarchy.

Modernizing the economy

The Fascist government encouraged industries, especially those of military value, such as metals and chemicals. Roads and railways were improved for the same reason. Marshy land was drained to increase wheat output. Electricity output tripled between 1920 and 1935 – but was still less than half what it was in Britain, a country with roughly the same population. In 1939 there were just 372,000 motor vehicles on the roads in Italy, compared with 2,527,000 in Britain. And in 1939 the average Italian's living standard only equalled what the average Briton had reached by 1800.

Fascists were attracted to speed and technology as symbols of power and progress. 'The Flying Duce' (below), named after Mussolini, was introduced in 1938 and could travel at 100 miles per hour.

Compromise with the Church

In 1929 the Lateran Accords settled quarrels between the Roman Catholic Church and the state dating back to 1870, when Italian soldiers had conquered the pope's territories and made Rome Italy's capital. The Accords recognized the Vatican as an independent state, paid generous compensation for its lost lands and confirmed Roman Catholicism as Italy's national religion. Young Mussolini had been very anti-clerical but, as a practical politician, he thought it wiser to make a friend of the pope. The Church regarded order under Mussolini as preferable to chaos or, worse still, communism.

The Pope

In 1926, when Mussolini survived the fourth attempt on his life, Pope Pius XI declared that

'This is a new sign that Mussolini has God's full protection.'

Later he denounced Fascism as

'a creed entirely given over to hate, to irreverence and to violence.'

Anti-Semitism

In 1937, Mussolini warned Italy's Jews to 'uphold Fascism or leave'. Following Italy's alliance with Germany, books by Jews were censored, anti-Semitic periodicals were permitted, and leading Jews were arrested. Jews found it hard to get work, but there was no brutal persecution to match the horrors of Nazi Germany. Later, during the war, when German forces tried to deport Italian Jews, the Italian army and authorities absolutely refused to cooperate and many Italians risked their lives to help them hide.

A new Caesar

Mussolini presented himself as a Julius Caesar reborn, renewing the glory of ancient Rome, making Italy admired, feared and prosperous, mistress once more of a great empire. In the 1930s he greatly increased military spending. Ethiopia was conquered in just seven months in 1935-36, for the loss of only 1,537 Italian lives – and tens of thousands of Ethiopian ones. When the League of Nations imposed trade sanctions on Italy as punishment for its aggression, Italy left the League.

November 1935: new subjects of the Italian empire, Ethiopians were taught to make the Fascist salute to portraits of Mussolini.

In July 1936 Mussolini sent 50,000 Italian 'volunteers' to Spain to support the army rebellion against the socialist government. The Spanish Civil War was a chance to develop military skills while supporting fellow fascists. In 1938 Mussolini aligned Italy with Hitler's Germany as an anti-communist power.

Crisis and collapse

In 1939 Italy invaded Albania. In 1940, fearful of being left behind by German victories, Mussolini ordered advances against Yugoslavia and Greece and in North Africa against the British. But Italy's effort in the Second World War was weakened by rivalries among

August 1938: King Victor Emmanel III and Mussolini (right) at army manoeuvres.

army, navy, airforce, militia and police forces, which Mussolini encouraged in order to increase his personal power as settler of disputes. Each, for example, had its own spies, but none shared information with the others.

Joining the war proved disastrous. It cost Italy a third of its national wealth. In Greece and Yugoslavia Italian forces became bogged down in guerrilla fighting. Britain reconquered all Italian territories in North and East Africa by 1942. Between 1940 and 1943 two-thirds of Italian shipping was sunk.

On 10 July 1943 Allied forces invaded Sicily. Defeat looked inevitable. On 24-25 July the Fascist Grand Council, meeting for the first time since war broke out, dismissed Mussolini. The king then had Mussolini arrested and made a leading soldier, Marshal Pietro Badoglio, prime minister. His government, mostly military men and government officials, changed sides to support the Allies. German paratroopers snatched Mussolini from prison to set up an 'Italian Social Republic', with a few remaining Fascist followers, at Salo, a small town in northern Italy. In reality this was only a German puppet state. German troops meanwhile fought a bitter rearguard action the length of Italy. 100,000 Italian partisans, particularly communist groups, harassed their retreat. 36,000 partisans died and 10,000 civilians were killed in German reprisals.

Count Galeazzo Ciano A death in the family

At 19, Ciano (1903-44) took part in the March on Rome. At 27, he married Mussolini's daughter, Edda. Mussolini put him in charge of press and propaganda and made him a member of the Fascist Grand Council. Ciano led a bomber squadron in the Ethiopian war and became foreign minister in 1936. Initially favouring war alongside Germany, he was dismayed by Italian defeats and pressed for peace with the Allies. He supported the dismissal of Mussolini. But when Badoglio's government charged him with corruption, he fled – only to be captured by pro-Mussolini partisans and German forces. He was tried for treason on Mussolini's personal order and shot.

The end

When Italy was torn between advancing Allies and retreating Germans, with its own army and partisan forces split and fighting on both sides, far more Italians – Catholics as well as communists – were willing to die to overthrow Fascism than to defend it. Mussolini's regime failed to create the 'New Man' who would give his life for a Fascist Italy. Most Italians, after all, had never been that interested in politics and simply tried to get on with their lives, more concerned about their families, homes, farms or jobs than political parades or speeches. The king and the pope remained as alternative symbols of authority. The contrast with Nazi SS units, fighting until they were wiped out, could not be greater. Italian Fascism seems to have been satisfied by the appearance of unity, energy and strength and ended up believing its own propaganda. The test of war proved to be a collision between dreams and harsh reality, exposing Fascism as a sham and a failure.

In April 1945 Mussolini tried to escape to Austria, disguised as a German soldier. He was caught and shot by communist partisans. His body was hung upside down in Milan for crowds to spit on.

Italian soldiers surrender when British forces attack the port of Bardia, Libya. Mussolini had called it a 'bastion of fascism'.

The post-war scene in Italy

Since 1946, when monarchy was replaced with a republic, Italy has had over 50 governments. But it has become prosperous and modern. Communists have been a major political force, governing cities such as Rome, Florence, Naples and Bologna. A neo-Fascist party, the *Movimento Sociale Italiano* (Italian Social Movement) was founded in 1956. It denies being anti-democratic but still plays on the failures of democratic politicians, demands new frontiers for Italy and calls for a national revival led by the young and strong. In 1994, re-established as the National Alliance, it formed part of a short-lived coalition government headed by media tycoon Silvio Berlusconi. Neo-Fascist splinter groups were also held responsible for terrorist bombings in 1969, 1974 and 1980. However, such attempts to create a state of crisis in which Fascism could again proclaim itself the guardian of order have significantly failed.

Racial Fascism Germany 1933-45

Like Italy, Germany was united by wars. Between 1864 and 1871 Schleswig-Holstein was taken from Denmark, Alsace and Lorraine were taken from France, and the King of Prussia was accepted as Kaiser (emperor) by the rulers of other German states. Unlike Italy, united Germany was an economic giant, with Europe's best-equipped army and a brand-new navy. Like Italy, Germany conquered colonies overseas. Unlike Italians, Germans had high average levels of education and rising incomes, and struck visitors as efficient and law-abiding. The new Germany mixed ancient and modern. Aristocrats dominated government and army, yet the country led the world in science and had Europe's first social security system.

After the First World War, the Treaty of Versailles set up new national states in the ruins of the Russian and Austro-Hungarian empires. The Treaty also gave pieces of German land to Belgium, France, Poland, Denmark and Lithuania; and said that the Rhineland, Ruhr and Saar should be occupied by the Allies for 15 years.

ESTONIA
LATVIA
LITHUANIA

Land lost by Germany
Land lost by Russia
Land lost by Austria-Hungary

N   Netherlands
L   Luxemburg

(Ger.) East Prussia

POLAND

USSR

Ruhr
GERMANY

N

BELGIUM
L

Rhine

Rhineland

Saar

CZECHOSLOVAKIA

FRANCE

SWITZ-ERLAND

AUSTRIA   HUNGARY

ROMANIA

Black Sea

YUGOSLAVIA

ITALY

BULGARIA

0   200   400 Km
0   125   250 Miles

Often silent and sulky as an individual, Hitler discovered that he had an electrifying talent as a platform speaker.

Defeat in the First World War

In June 1914 a Serb assassinated the Crown Prince of Austria-Hungary. A month later, the Central Powers – Germany, Austria-Hungary and Ottoman Turkey – found themselves at war with France, Britain, Russia, Belgium and Serbia, later joined by Italy and the USA. The two sides were locked into confrontation by their alliances, and the war dragged on until the Central Powers gave up, near exhaustion.

Disgrace

In 1919, politicians meeting at Weimar adopted a new constitution making Germany a democratic republic. The same politicians signed the Versailles Treaty, the First World War peace settlement. This treaty blamed Germany for starting the war and forced the country to pay huge reparations. It laid down that Germany must give up its colonies and 13 per cent of its home territory and agree to demilitarize the Rhineland, limit the army to 100,000 and have no airforce. All these humiliations were accepted – although no Allied soldier had even set foot on German soil.

The Nazis

Adolf Hitler, who had joined the army in 1914, was stunned by Germany's defeat. After 1918 he stayed in the army, spying on political groups, and the following year

The young Hitler From failure to hero

Adolf Hitler (1889-1945) was born Austrian, not German. A failed art student, he drifted to Vienna, then Munich. Lacking education, money, family and friends, he still dreamed of greatness for himself. He volunteered immediately war broke out in 1914. The German army gave him order, discipline and comradeship. Hitler won the Iron Cross twice, but was never promoted beyond corporal because his superiors thought him no leader.

he became the seventh member of the German Workers' Party. He discovered an unsuspected talent for public speaking, became the party's leader and changed its name to National Socialist German Workers' Party – Nazi, for short. Hitler insisted that Germany had not been defeated in battle but had been betrayed by the 'November Criminals' who signed the Versailles Treaty. Germany's post-war shame and chaos were blamed on communists, socialists, liberals and Jews. Because he needed to attract workers away from their loyalty to trade unions, Hitler also attacked big business for not taking better care of employees. He found eager listeners among ex-soldiers and the unemployed.

> ## How to establish an idea
> Hitler understood the power of propaganda and organization:
>
> *'Only constant repeating will finally succeed in imprinting an idea on the memory of the crowd.' (Mein Kampf)*

A turning point

In 1923 French troops occupied Germany to enforce payment of reparations. Inflation destroyed Germany's currency, wiping out savings. Communists attempted a rising in Hamburg. Against this background Hitler founded a paramilitary force, the *Sturmabteilung* (SA, Storm Battalion), known as 'Brownshirts' from their uniform. Like Italian *squadristi*, SA squads were to beat up opponents and break up communist or socialist meetings. A typical poster for the SA showed its members as clean-cut, muscular members of a tug-of-war team, over the slogan 'SA service – pull together for Comradeship, Endurance, Strength!'

On the move again: Stormtroopers in Munich, 1923.

In November, inspired by Mussolini's 'March on Rome', Hitler launched an uprising from a Munich beer hall, supported by war hero General Erich Ludendorff and fighter ace Hermann Goering. Police shot 16 Nazis dead. Hitler was sentenced to five years in prison but served only nine months, which he used to dictate *Mein Kampf* (*My Struggle*).

Mein Kampf

In his book, Hitler repeated the same themes ceaselessly:

☛ Humans belong to separate races which should be kept 'pure' and not interbreed. Struggle between races moves history. The blonde 'Aryan' race of northern Europe creates the superior culture. Other races are valuable only to serve Aryans. Jews destroy culture.

'All those who are not racially pure are simply waste.'

☛ Germans, the purest Aryans, will rule the world. Germany must crush communists, democrats and Jews who weaken it. Germany must take in all Germans outside its borders and conquer eastern Europe as *Lebensraum* (living space) for Germans to create ideal Aryan communities.

'Germany will either be a world power or not exist at all.'

☛ Hitler will make this vision happen. Democratic parliaments make quarrels and weakness. Government is about leadership and loyalty, not discussion and compromise. Obedience to an inspired *Führer* (leader) heading a disciplined movement of Germany's fittest and finest will bring unity and strength.

Which way for Weimar?

Hitler believed in his destiny but his rise to power was not inevitable. Having failed to seize power by force, he turned to building the Nazis as a political party. He had only contempt for democracy, but election publicity could attract members.

Germany prospered from 1925, joined the League of Nations and saw French occupation troops depart. In the 1928 *Reichstag* (parliament) elections, Nazis got only 2.6 per cent of the votes. In 1929 the party had only 176,000 members. Then came the collapse of world trade, financial panic and mass unemployment.

Economic chaos opened the door to political opportunity. In 1930 Nazis polled 18.3 per cent, becoming the second biggest party. In 1931 the jobless passed 4,000,000. A Nazi election poster of the period shows a crowd of haggard, jobless men beneath the slogan 'Our Last Hope – Hitler'. In 1932 Nazis registered 33.1 per cent, becoming the biggest party, although Hitler was beaten for the presidency by aged war hero General Paul von Hindenburg.

The Nazi dictatorship

Like Mussolini, Hitler owed power to a head of state weary of unstable government and fearful of chaos. President Hindenburg appointed Hitler Chancellor (prime minister) of a coalition government in January 1933. In February the Reichstag building burned down. Hitler blamed communists and got emergency powers from the Reichstag. In July the Nazis

The Nazi Party claimed to be building up society with work, freedom and bread, while the plans of its political rivals would bring destruction.

SS supermen

Founded in 1923 as Hitler's personal bodyguard, the SS (Schutzstaffeln – protection squads) numbered only hundreds when Heinrich Himmler (1900-45) took command in 1929. By 1933 there were 209,000 SS members. Himmler wanted them to be Nazism's elite, physically perfect Aryans, fanatically devoted to Hitler. The SS took control of the police, secret police and concentration camps.

Some divisions of the Waffen-SS (armed SS) were formed from non-German 'Aryans'. North European Latvians (3 divisions), Estonians (2) and Dutch (2) were clearly 'cousins' in the same Teutonic racial family. But Croats (2), Ukrainians (2) and Belorussians (1) were Slavs, and therefore technically 'Untermenschen' (subhumans), as were Muslim Albanians (2). So, in reality, Nazi leaders valued willing soldiers above their own racial theories.

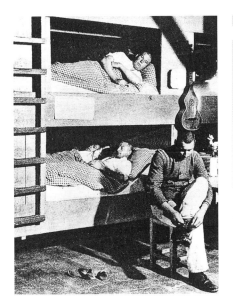

This picture of bunks at the concentration camp in Dachau appeared in a Nazi newspaper, which explained that the camp managers encouraged prisoners to 'beautify' their rooms as well as keep them clean.

The madhouse

In 1933, Sir Walter Rumbold, British Ambassador to Germany, remarked:

'Many of us ... have a feeling that we are living in a country where fantastic hooligans and eccentrics have got the upper hand.'

became the only legal party. This began the *Gleichschaltung* (streamlining) of any possible opposition. Even the Boy Scouts were dissolved into the Hitler Youth. Anti-Nazis – communists, Catholics, union leaders, journalists – were sent to concentration camps for 'political education' (beatings and torture).

In June 1934, Hitler used the SS to murder SA leaders in the 'Night of the Long Knives'. He did this because some of the SA still believed in his early attacks on big business, whereas now he needed big business to re-arm Germany. The murders made clear that no opposition was allowed. The public was told that 77 plotters (in fact it was hundreds) had been executed for treason. In August 1934 Hindenburg died and Hitler proclaimed himself *Führer*, merging the powers of Chancellor and President.

The SS oath

'We swear to you, Adolf Hitler, loyalty and bravery as leader and chancellor of the German Reich. We vow to you and to the principles laid down by you obedience to the point of death. So help us God!'

Warfare and welfare

By 1935 Hitler felt strong enough to defy the Versailles Treaty, reintroducing conscription and beginning to build an airforce. He believed, correctly, that the memory of the First World War would make France, Britain and their allies accept almost anything to avoid another. In 1936 he sent German forces into the Rhineland and to support the army revolt in Spain.

Meanwhile the 1935 'Nuremberg Laws' forbade Jews to marry Aryans. Jewish doctors and teachers were allowed to treat and teach only other Jews. A Jew was defined by blood, not religion, as anyone – including Christians – with one or more Jewish grandparent. Of Germany's 500,000 Jews, half emigrated by 1938, abandoning businesses, homes and belongings.

Tens of thousands suffered from the Nazi takeover, but millions benefited. Rearmament and the building of *Autobahnen* (motorways) created jobs. Loyal Nazis were rewarded with posts in the party or with businesses or homes confiscated from Jews.

Alfred Rosenberg
Philosopher of Nazism

Rosenberg was born in Russia in 1893. After the 1917 Revolution, he went to Munich, joined the Nazi party and became editor of its newspaper, the *Völkischer Beobachter* (*Racial Observer*). When Hitler was imprisoned after the Munich rising, he made Rosenberg temporary party leader – thinking him too incompetent to take it over for himself. Rosenberg later set himself to become Nazism's philosopher. He wrote that Germans were descended from an ancient Nordic race who once inhabited a semi-Arctic continent, now disappeared; from this race Germans inherited a mission to dominate the world. Hitler denied Rosenberg any real power, but he was tried for war crimes at Nuremberg and hanged in 1946.

Winterhilfe (winter help) campaigns collected money and food for the old and needy. The *Kraft durch Freude* (Strength through Joy) programme organized cheap trips and holidays. The Berlin Olympics were a showcase of Aryan superiority in 1936. Although a black American athlete, Jesse Owens, stole the show, German competitors topped the medals table.

Germany's new motorways made it possible to move troops much faster. They could also serve as emergency landing-strips.

Homecoming

Hitler's Germany was to be '*Ein Reich, Ein Volk, Ein Führer*' (One Realm, One People, One Leader) – all Germans in a single state. Aided by Austrian Nazis, German troops took over Hitler's native country in 1938. In 1939 Hitler bullied Czechoslovakia into giving up its Sudetenland frontier region, with 2,000,000 Germans, and seized the former German port of Memel from Lithuania. Attacking Poland in 1939 would bring more Germans 'home' and add *Lebensraum* in the East. It began the Second World War.

Victories and defeat

At first Hitler won unbroken victories. But in 1941 he invaded the USSR and declared war on the USA. In 1942 a huge German army surrendered at Stalingrad and another was beaten in North Africa. In 1943 Italy changed from ally to enemy. In 1944 the Allies invaded France and a German army officers' plot came close to assassinating Hitler himself.

The Nazi Women's Labour Service at a rally in Nuremberg.

Fascism and Nazism – the differences

Fascism lasted almost twice as long in Italy as Nazism did in Germany. Mussolini made himself a dictator by stages over several years. The break with the past was more gradual and less complete than in Nazi Germany. The monarchy remained and the Roman Church was not attacked.

Hitler became a dictator more quickly than Mussolini. There was no German monarchy as an alternative focus of national loyalty. The Nazis were openly hostile to religion and actually tried to revive pagan beliefs and ceremonies. Racism – notably anti-Semitism – was central to Hitler's programme for a new Germany. And whereas Mussolini aimed to settle Italians in an overseas empire (though little was done in practice about this), Hitler's opposite priority was to bring Germans in neighbouring states under Nazi rule. Nazism was, above all, far more violent than Italian Fascism and, because Germany had so many more people and bigger, better industries, Nazism was more destructive, both to Germany and to the world as a whole.

Nazi puppet states

Out of Austria-Hungary's ruins at the end of the First World War had come two new multi-ethnic states: Czechoslovakia, where the Czechs were more powerful and prosperous than the Slovaks; and Yugoslavia, where Orthodox Serbs were resented by Catholic Croats. These two states were so-called allies of Nazi Germany, but Nazi policy played on their divisions and treated them little better than enemies.

After the Nazi take-over of Czechoslovakia in March 1939, Slovakia became 'independent' with a Catholic priest, Monsignor Josef Tiso (1887-1947), as president. In practice, it was occupied by German troops and exploited for Germany's war effort. Tiso's Nazi-style regime – one political party, paramilitary force and youth movement – co-operated with Nazi genocide, sending 100,000 Slovak Jews to death and 50,000 Slovak troops to the Eastern Front, where half died. A Slovak army revolt in August 1944 cost another 25,000 lives before the Soviet army drove the Nazis out. Tiso was tried and hanged by his own countrymen. By 1948 Slovakia was again part of Czechoslovakia, under communist rule. After communism's collapse, Slovakia became independent peacefully in 1993, by means of a 'velvet divorce' from the Czech Republic.

After the Nazi conquest of Yugoslavia in April 1941, an 'independent' Croatia was established and exploited in a similar way to Slovakia. It even paid for German and Italian occupation troops. Croat leader Ante Pavelic (1889-1959) concentrated on 'ethnic cleansing', killing some 300,000 Serbs before fleeing into exile. Croatia became part of Yugoslavia again, also under communist rule. Following Yugoslavia's break-up, Croatia declared independence in 1991. Inter-ethnic fighting split it into Croat-controlled and Serb-controlled areas.

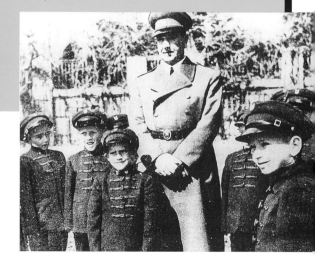

Ante Pavelic on a visit to a school in Croatia. Like Hitler, he often had himself photographed with children, looking to be an interested protector of the new generation.

The Final Solution

Until 1939 Nazi policy encouraged Jewish emigration. Wartime conquests brought millions more Jews under Nazi rule. Forced emigration was impossible in a war situation. The next step was systematic mass-murder. The German army pushing east in June 1941 was followed by 3,000 SS who killed 600,000 Jews by November, aided by local Lithuanians and Ukrainians.

Children at a labour camp near Lodz, Poland.

Jews in Nazi-occupied countries were sent to concentration camps or used as slave labour in SS factories. The last phase of the 'Final Solution' of the 'Jewish question' was to transport Jews far from their homes to purpose-built death-camps. Told they were being 'resettled', victims usually cooperated until it was too late to escape. Bulgaria, Finland and Italy, Germany's allies, refused to hand over their Jewish citizens. Occupied Denmark smuggled almost all of its 5,500 Jews into Sweden. Over 6,000,000 Jews were murdered, plus hundreds of thousands of gypsies, homosexuals and mentally or physically disabled people who did not fit the image of the Aryan 'superman'.

Fear creates silence

Protestant pastor Martin Niemöller survived eight years in concentration camps. In 1961 he became President of the World Council of Churches. He commented:

'The Nazis came for the communists and I didn't speak up because I was not a communist. Then they came for the Jews and I didn't speak up because I was not a Jew. Then they came for the trade unionists and I didn't speak up because I was not a trade unionist. Then they came for the Catholics and I was a Protestant so I didn't speak up. Then they came for me ... By that time there was no one to speak up for anyone.'

Defeat and division

Hitler shot himself in the ruins of Berlin on 30 April 1945. He had constantly predicted that the Nazi regime would be a 'Thousand Year Reich'. It collapsed within ten days of his suicide. Germany was divided into US, British, French and Russian occupation zones. The first three were reunited as a democratic Federal Republic of Germany (West Germany) in 1949. The Russian zone became the communist-ruled German Democratic Republic (East Germany). After the collapse of communism in the USSR, East and West Germany reunited in 1990.

Neo-Nazism

After the Second World War, West Germany paid reparations to surviving Jews and banned Nazism in any form. But neo-Nazi groups have re-established themselves behind front organizations such as publishing houses or so-called research institutes, issuing pamphlets denying that the Holocaust ever happened. In 1980, *Deutsche Aktionsgruppen* (German Action Groups) bombed refugee hostels, killing two inmates. In 1981 their leader, Manfred Roeder, was imprisoned for 13 years for encouraging such acts.

A photograph of two Turkish teenagers who died when their home in Solingen, Germany, was firebombed by right-wing extremists in 1993.

Since reunification there has been a revival of neo-Nazism in former East Germany, mainly consisting of attacks on immigrants and refugees. The East German communist regime simply ignored the Nazi past of most of its own people, and so they never experienced the public heart-searching that happened in West Germany through public debate, the churches and education. East German resentment at the gap between local living standards and those of former West Germany continues to fuel discontent, especially among unemployed youth, who pick on refugees maintained at public expense as a target for their hatreds. Anti-immigrant feeling has also become a strong force in Austrian politics.

Fascism's Followers

The fascist regimes in Italy and Germany inspired copy-cat movements in other countries, which had their own distinctive problems arising from defeat, poverty, tensions between regions or classes, or the challenge of coping with recent independence or changed frontiers. The scope for, and aims of, fascist action therefore varied in each case. Italy and Germany seemed to represent successful approaches to national challenges. Their aggressiveness in foreign affairs also made some states want to become their allies, as well as their imitators, either for self-protection or because they hoped to gain by it.

Doing the same is not imitating

'They say we are imitators ... but since Germany and Italy have turned back on themselves and have totally rediscovered themselves, why should we say that Spain is imitating them in its quest to find a way back to herself? ... by reproducing the achievement of the Italians or Germans we will become more Spanish than we have ever been.'
(José Antonio Primo de Rivera, 1935)

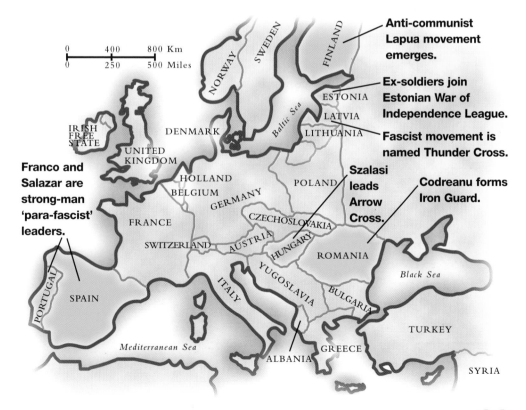

Anti-communist Lapua movement emerges.

Ex-soldiers join Estonian War of Independence League.

Fascist movement is named Thunder Cross.

Szalasi leads Arrow Cross.

Codreanu forms Iron Guard.

Franco and Salazar are strong-man 'para-fascist' leaders.

The 'strong man' leaders who emerged in these countries might best be termed 'para-fascist' – their regimes often looked fascist and they were willing to cooperate with fascist powers; but, recognizing the revolutionary power of genuine fascist movements, they tolerated them only so long as they could control them. When a fascist movement threatened the stability and authority the leader was trying to impose, it was either taken over or smashed.

Fascism absorbed – Spain

By the 1920s Spain, once the greatest power in Europe, was one of its most backward countries. The Catholic Church, the army and the landowning class dominated a nation of poor peasants. In 1923 widespread disorder led King Alfonso XIII to encourage General Miguel Primo de Rivera (1870-1930) to rule as dictator, following the conservative slogan 'Country, Religion, Monarchy'.

FRANCE
ANDORRA
Corunna
Santander Bilbao
Barcelona
Saragossa
Salamanca
MENORCA
MADRID
MALLORCA
Toledo
Valencia
PORTUGAL
IBIZA
Alicante
Nationalist zone
Cordoba
Republican zone
Seville
Malaga
Granada
Cadiz
SPANISH MOROCCO
0   250 Km
0   150 Miles

Dissolving the *Cortes* (parliament) as corrupt and inefficient, the general ruled by military law. Although he crushed three attempts to overthrow his government by force in 1926, and ended an unpopular colonial war in Morocco in 1927, he failed to win the support of the middle classes for his *Union Patriotica* party. His reliance on landlord support blocked the land reforms needed to end peasant distress. As public finances slid into chaos in 1929, he lost the crucial support of the army and resigned from ill-health in 1930. Alfonso fled into exile in 1931 and Spain became a republic.

The division of Spain into Nationalist and Republican zones, in July 1936.

Rebels in Asturias in 1934 were arrested by civil guards.

José Antonio Primo de Rivera
Founder of the Falange

Lawyer José Antonio Primo de Rivera was the son of the former dictator. In 1933 he founded the Falange as a political party, to carry forward his father's ideas in a forward-looking, rather than conservative, way. Falangists stressed Spanish tradition and the superiority of nation over class or region. Falange means 'phalanx', a close-packed military formation used in ancient Greece – hence a symbol of unity and strength. José Antonio spoke out fiercely against the left-wing Popular Front government of the republic, which dissolved his party, imprisoned him and, after the outbreak of civil war, executed him for treason. Anti-republicans regarded him as a martyr.

Instability continued as Catalans and Basques demanded autonomy, anti-clericals attacked priests and nuns, and communists led a miners' strike in Asturias. In 1934 Catalonia, the region around Barcelona, declared independence, but this was crushed by government forces. When the communists were excluded from government in February 1936, they also began an uprising.

In 1937, General Francisco Franco merged the Falange and similar groups to create a 'Traditionalist Spanish Falange' – with the stress on Traditionalist – as Spain's only legal party. From 1939 to 1942, he used the Grand Council of the Falange to pass laws creating a dictatorship with himself as *Caudillo* (leader). In organization and outward style,

Civil War in Spain, 1936-39

In 1936, the Spanish army rebelled against the republican government, rapidly seizing most of southern and western Spain. Other countries pledged neutrality, but allowed volunteers to join in. Sixty thousand came from Britain, France, the USA and other democracies to fight for the republic. The USSR sent air support and technical advisers. Nazi Germany sent 25,000 regular troops, pretending to be volunteers, to fight for the rebels. Fascist Italy sent 30,000. Genuine pro-rebel volunteer forces of a few hundred came from Ireland and Romania. Both sides regularly massacred prisoners. At least half a million, possibly twice as many, died before the war ended in 1939 with the army's victory under General Franco.

Franco's dictatorship resembled Fascist Italy, but Franco aimed to stabilize Spain rather than modernize it. The Falange became a powerless talking-shop for the few who took fascism seriously as a revolutionary philosophy. Like the old order, Franco's power rested on the support of the armed forces, Church and landowners, backed up by censorship and secret police.

November 1936: boys in Irun formed a fascist organization.

During the Second World War Franco sent Spanish volunteers, the Blue Legion, to fight with Germany on the Eastern Front against the USSR, but otherwise he kept Spain neutral because Hitler would not let

him take over France's colonies in North Africa. The defeat of the fascist powers in 1945 caused Franco to downgrade the Falange even further, in order to improve Spain's relations with the USA and Western democracies. Spanish isolation and backwardness lasted into the 1960s, when kissing in public or wearing a bikini were still illegal. In 1969 Franco declared the grandson of Alfonso XIII, Prince Juan Carlos, as his successor. Franco's death in 1975 was followed by an orderly transition to democracy. In 1977 the Falange was finally disbanded and the Communist Party legalized. In 1980 Basques and Catalans were given regional parliaments.

Francisco Franco Bahamonde A modest dictator

Franco (1892-1975) was a career soldier who became Europe's youngest general in 1926. He never trusted politicians, but believed in the military virtues of order and discipline. As a leader, he lacked personal magnetism to the point of dullness, but he always kept a firm grip on power. A master of manipulating rivalries, he never hesitated from brutality towards opponents.

Spanish and other European members of Neo-Nazi parties at a rally in memory of General Franco in Madrid, November 1991.

Portuguese dictator dismisses fascism

As finance minister, Antonio de Oliveira Salazar (1889-1970) saved Portugal's finances when world trade collapsed in 1929. After becoming prime minister, he proclaimed the *Estado Novo* (New State) in 1933-34. He ruled as dictator, supervising all official appointments, until a stroke forced him to resign in 1968.

Educated for the Catholic priesthood, Salazar lived simply and had no interest in a personality cult or in typically fascist parades and propaganda. His rule was supported by the Church, the army, landowners and businessmen and a feared secret police. His *Uniao Nacional* (National Union) was the only permitted party. He saw Portugal's fascist movement, the 25,000-strong blue-shirted National Syndicalists, as potentially disruptive and dissolved it in 1934.

Fascism, fatal ally – Hungary and Romania

Hungary's situation after the First World War was similar to Germany's: the monarchy ended, lands lost, and revolution threatening. It became briefly a democratic republic, then communist, before Admiral Horthy drove out the communists to establish a Kingdom of Hungary with himself as Regent (1920-44). Horthy aimed to reverse the post-war treaties which cost Hungary two-thirds of its former lands and peoples, including 3,000,000 Hungarians.

Hungary's wounded pride and strong local anti-Semitism created possible supporters for fascist movements, but the only significant one was the Party of National Will, founded in 1935 by ex-army officer Ferenc Szalasi (1897-1946) and renamed the Arrow Cross party in 1937. The Arrow Cross supported Horthy in reclaiming lost lands, but he thought it might challenge his authority, imprisoned Szalasi (1938-49) and banned the movement.

Horthy disliked Hitler but by allying Hungary with Germany and introducing anti-Jewish laws he regained Hungarian-inhabited parts of Slovakia and Romania in 1938-40. In 1941, believing that Germany would win the war, Horthy sent his army to support the invasion of Russia. After two-thirds of the Hungarian army had died there, Horthy tried to make a separate peace with the Allies. The Germans imprisoned him and put Szalasi in his place. He lasted six months, leaving with the Nazis as they were pushed out of Hungary by Soviet and Romanian troops. Szalasi was captured by US troops in Germany and returned to Hungary where the communist-led government had him tried and shot. The USA allowed Horthy exile in Portugal.

Nuremberg 1938: Hitler's deputy, Rudolf Hess (left) looks on as Admiral Horthy of Hungary (1868-1957) is welcomed to the city with a glass of its traditional drink.

Romania, unlike Hungary, had doubled its territories by siding with the Allies in the First World War. However, the country had been thoroughly looted by the Germans and, as a result of its new frontiers, it gained many new Jewish inhabitants as well as other minorities. Politics was confused by conflicts between many parties, none capable of becoming dominant and the communists threatening revolution. The post-war situation was therefore highly unstable.

Romanian fascism was created by Corneliu Codreanu (1899-1938), who blamed Jews for all Romania's problems. In 1927 he founded the paramilitary Legion of the Archangel Michael as a terrorist elite, and in 1930 he enlarged it into a mass movement, the Iron Guard. In 1933 Guardists assassinated Liberal Prime Minister Duca. Banned as a result, the Guard immediately re-invented itself as *Totul Pentra Tara* ('All for the Country').

By 1937 the Guard was Romania's third largest party, after the Conservatives and Liberals. King Carol II (reigned 1930-40), an admirer of Mussolini, saw it as a threat because he did not control it himself. In 1938 Carol made himself dictator at the head of a National Renaissance Front, which he intended to be the only legal party. Codreanu and 13 of his followers were 'shot while trying to escape' – i.e. murdered in prison.

In 1940 Germany and the USSR together took 40 per cent of Romania's territory and half its population. Guardists blamed Carol, forcing him to abdicate in favour of his teenage son, Michael (reigned 1940-47). Real power passed to General Ion Antonescu (1882-1946), another admirer of Mussolini, who took the title *Conducator*, the Romanian equivalent of *Duce*, and aimed to recover some of Romania's lost lands by siding with Germany. He appointed Guard leaders to government and made their leader, Horia Sima,

deputy prime minister. Guardists then murdered 64 politicians and generals whom they considered enemies of Romania. Still they threatened further action. So, in January 1941 Antonescu, following Hitler's advice, crushed the Guard in two days of bloodshed.

As Hitler's ally, Antonescu sent 30 Romanian divisions to fight in Russia where they suffered huge losses. Romanians blamed Antonescu. As the Soviet army reached Romania's frontier in 1944, King Michael arrested him and declared war on Germany. Antonescu, tried for war crimes, was shot in 1946. By 1947 communists had forced Michael into exile and taken over government.

Ion Antonescu of Romania makes a speech, with his Iron Guard in front of him and a portrait of Horia Sima behind.

Anti-communist fascism – the Baltic States

Until the First World War, Finland, Estonia and Latvia were within the Russian empire. All then fought against communist Russia to claim their independence, an experience which left many veterans anti-communist. There was also hostility in the states to non-Baltic local minorities, such as Germans, Russians and Jews. As small independent republics the Baltic states were sandwiched between powerful neighbours. This permanent threat to their security, plus the impact of the world depression after 1929, made all of them vulnerable to the appeal of strong-man rule and the ideal of a racially 'pure' nation, united in its own defence.

Finland

In 1929 a nationwide anti-communist movement called Lapua emerged under Vihtori Kosola, who modelled himself on Mussolini and encouraged terrorist acts against communist organizations and individuals. When the Finnish government banned communism, this satisfied enough of Lapua's supporters to end it as a mass movement, but Kosola then wanted to challenge parliamentary rule itself. A Lapua militia rising in 1932 was easily crushed and Lapua itself was banned. Hardcore supporters immediately formed a People's Patriotic Movement, aiming to expand the nation as a Greater Finland. This re-formed movement attracted 100,000 members, including a youth movement which wore black shirts and blue ties. The movement lost support after 1936 as Finland prospered, but some of its leaders served in government when Finland was Germany's ally (1941-43). It was banned again after the Soviet invasion of 1944.

Estonia

The Estonian War of Independence League (EVL), established in 1929, appealed to the nation's youth to create a more unified, anti-communist Estonia. As a movement of ex-soldiers it was, not surprisingly, military in style, patriotic in outlook and suspicious of party politicians. But, unlike true fascist movements, the EVL was neither revolutionary nor violent. Keeping within the law, in 1933 the EVL won 73 per cent support for a new constitution to create a stronger presidency. President Konstantin Päts, a hero of the War of Independence and admirer of Hitler, used his new powers to ban the EVL. He ruled without parliament while a new constitution was drafted, creating an Italian Fascist-style chamber effectively under his control. EVL propaganda chief Hjalmar Mae served as head of government during the Nazi occupation of Estonia (1941-44).

Latvia

In 1934 Latvia's democracy was replaced by dictatorship under Karlis Ulmanis, leader of the Farmers' Union party. Ulmanis's government was partly modelled on Mussolini's but was opposed by the local fascist movement, the grey-shirted Fire Cross, later renamed Thunder Cross. Ulmanis banned the movement and, when it continued in secret, arrested many members in 1935 and 1937. He also suppressed the local branch of the Baltic Brotherhood, recruited from local Germans who wanted Latvia to become part of the Nazi Reich. During the Nazi occupation of Latvia Thunder Cross members joined death squads murdering local Jews and served in a Latvian division of the German army fighting the USSR.

Latvia for Latvians

'In a Latvian Latvia the question of minorities will not exist. Only Latvians will rule themselves and the other nations which live here ... Our God, our belief, our life's meaning, our goal is the Latvian nation: whoever is against its welfare is our enemy ... Estonians and Lithuanians ... for us are not foreign peoples ... Jews, Germans, Poles, Russians. All of them are non-Latvians and in a Latvian Latvia there is no place for them.'
(Gustav Celmins, Thunder Cross leader, 1933)

Fascist movements on the fringe of Europe were in each case only components of complex political situations. None became strong enough to dominate those situations, although their extremism and willingness to use violence could at times give them influence out of proportion to their numbers. When they received support from the Italy or Germany they admired, it was always intended to serve Italian or German interests rather than their own and they were readily sacrificed when interests conflicted. By taking over or destroying fascist movements within their borders, para-fascist leaders ironically paid them the compliment of recognizing their revolutionary potential – before defusing it.

Fascism's Failures

Fascist movements appeared in established democracies as well as in countries where democracy was weak or non-existent. Wherever the public kept its faith in democratic politics throughout periods of crisis, fascism remained little more than a noisy nuisance. Failing to command a mass following, most fascist movements in sound democracies proved to be petty bands of misfits attracted to would-be 'strong men' with an unreal sense of personal destiny. Only when war introduced an external element in the shape of Nazi occupation did fascist movements have the opportunity to share power and, even then, only so long as the occupation lasted.

Oswald Mosley and two supporters hoist the flag of the British Union of Fascists at its offices in Great George Street, London, a minute's walk from the Houses of Parliament.

Man of destiny? – Britain

As a fiercely ambitious young MP, Sir Oswald Mosley (1896-1980), an upper-class war hero, had changed from Conservative to Independent to Labour. In 1931 he left the Labour government, when it rejected his plans to fight unemployment, founded his own 'New

Party' and lost his seat in parliament in the next year's election. After visiting Mussolini, who offered him secret funding to promote fascism in Britain, Mosley merged the New Party into a British Union of Facsists (BUF) in 1932.

Tall and handsome, with a commanding voice, Mosley attracted people who thought that Britain needed 'a bit of discipline'. His message – 'Britain for the British' – was vague enough to mean anything from 'Trade with Britain's empire' to 'Down with the Jews'. Mosley was not personally anti-Jewish, but believed his movement needed a hate-object and Jews were convenient for this purpose. BUF 'Blackshirts' were created to fight Jewish and communist activists who interrupted his meetings. Street fights got newspaper headlines, giving the tiny movement much-needed publicity. Membership peaked at 50,000 in 1934.

Fascists during their march through East London, 4 October 1936.

Open Blackshirt brutality at a rally that year rebounded on the BUF as the public was horrified by their violence.

On 4 October 1936 a BUF column of 1,900, protected by thousands of police, tried marching through London's largely Jewish East End. It was a deliberately provocative act and 100,000 locals turned back the marchers with bricks and milk bottles in the 'Battle of Cable Street'. The government hastily passed a Public Order Act, banning political uniforms and increasing police powers to stop marches threatening public order. The BUF dwindled rapidly. In 1940 over a thousand members, including Mosley, were imprisoned as possible pro-Nazi traitors. Most were later released as harmless.

Police remove one of the barricades (made with an overturned lorry) which were erected to stop the Fascist marchers, in the 'Battle of Cable Street'.

In later life, Mosley lived in exile in France. He tried unsuccessfully to re-enter British politics by exploiting racist feeling against Commonwealth immigrants. Mosley's genuine talents were perverted by his delusion that Britain needed 'saving' and that he was its destined saviour.

"Blackshirt battle hymn

The marching song of the Blackshirts, written by poet and member E. D. Randell, was sung to the tune of the Horst Wessel Lied, the Nazi anthem:

'Comrades: the voice of the dead battalions
Of those who fell that Britain might be great,
Join in our song, for they still march in spirit with us
And urge us on to gain the Fascist State!'

⭐ Looking for a fight? – Ireland

Ireland's 'Blueshirt' movement or Army Comrades Association was founded in 1932 and renamed the National Guard in 1933 when ex-police chief Eoin O'Duffy (1892-1944) took it over as a Christian, anti-communist force to 'promote and maintain social order'. Most Blueshirts were, like O'Duffy himself, ex-IRA veterans of Ireland's war for independence from Britain. Blueshirt thinking was more influenced by Catholicism than by Mussolini and was traditionalist rather than revolutionary. In practice, Blueshirts promoted much disorder and in August 1933 were outlawed. Within days O'Duffy merged the movement with two other groups to form *Fine Gael* (United Ireland) – which he left within a year to found the openly fascist 'Greenshirt' National Corporate Party. In 1936-37 he led a volunteer Irish Brigade for Franco in Spain and retired from politics on his return. Without him the Greenshirts faded away. Fine Gael became one of Ireland's main democratic political parties.

General Eoin O'Duffy addresses a meeting of Blushirts near Cork.

Marshal Pétain, aged 90, at his trial in July 1945.

Too many cooks – France

Between the First and Second World Wars France had 44 different governments under 20 different prime ministers. Scandals and corruption were as common in parliament as riots and strikes on the streets. French fascists were neutralized both by the much stronger communists and by their own internal divisions and rivalries. The various groupings of fascists proved better at discussing everything than doing anything.

In 1940 France accepted German occupation and a pro-Nazi regime was established under aged war hero Marshal Pétain. Its police and officials enthusiastically arrested French Jews for deportation and death. Clearly, French support for fascist racism was present, even if would-be fascist saviours of France waited for the republic's collapse before wielding power to serve its destroyers.

Marshal Philippe Pétain Hero or victim?

After an unspectacular army career, Pétain (1856-1951) was transformed into a national hero by his defence of Verdun in 1916. Minister of War in 1934 and ambassador to Spain in 1939, he was recalled to government as France faced defeat in 1940. The day after becoming prime minister, he asked Germany for an armistice, then abolished the French republic and made himself head of state. Parties and unions were banned. Until November 1942, while German forces occupied the north and west of France, Pétain governed the rest from Vichy. Then German troops occupied the whole country and Pétain became a powerless figurehead. Taken to Germany in August 1944, he refused to join a pro-Nazi French government in exile. However, after the war he was tried and condemned to death for collaboration. In view of his age, he was imprisoned until death instead.

Fascism in Norway

In 1933, ex-soldier and politician Vidkun Quisling (1887-1945) founded the *Nasjonal Samling* (National Union), an anti-communist movement which looked to restore Norway to the greatness of its Viking days. Writer Knut Hamsun (1859-1952) shared Quisling's fascination with Norway's peasant heritage and hatred of modern city life. They hoped an alliance of 'Nordic' peoples – including the British – would defeat the worldwide threat represented by communists and Jews. Few ordinary Norwegians were persuaded by this

vision and Quisling's party collapsed in 1936. When the Nazis occupied Norway, Quisling organized an NS government to collaborate with them, serving as prime minister (1942-45) until their defeat. He was then arrested by the restored Norwegian government, tried and shot for treason. His name has passed into English (a quisling) to mean traitorous collaborator.

Burning a picture of the Norwegian fascist, Vidkun Quisling.

A house divided – Belgium

1930s Belgium was divided between the Walloon French-speaking minority, who dominated business and politics, and the Flemish-speaking majority, who felt they were missing out. In 1931, Flemish extremists formed the *Verbond van Dietsche Nationalsolidaristen* (Union of Dutch National Comrades) to promote Flemish interests.

French-speaking Léon Degrelle (1906-94) founded the Rex party in 1936, to attack communism and parliamentary corruption and reach an understanding with the Flemish. It took its name from Christus Rex – Christ the King. Rexists paraded with brooms to show they wanted to sweep Belgium clean. Rex grew quickly at first, then lost popularity just as quickly. Degrelle's Flemish followers broke away to join the *Vlaamsche National Verbond* (Flemish National Union). After the Nazis invaded Belgium in 1940, Degrelle made Rex an openly pro-Nazi party, formed a Walloon legion for the German SS and himself commanded them in Russia.

Democracy was swiftly restored in post-war Belgium, where, as in Sweden, the Netherlands and Switzerland, the possibility of a communist takeover had been too unlikely to frighten people into losing faith in parliamentary politics or tolerating violence on the streets. But rivalries among many small parties and the division between Flemings and Walloons continue to dominate Belgian politics to the present.

Partial fascisms – the USA

The USA's democracy tolerated a number of movements with fascist tendencies, but none seriously threatened democratic politics as a whole. The largest was the Ku Klux Klan (KKK), which revived rapidly in the 1920s to reach 2,000,000 members. Another was the pro-Nazi Friends of the New Germany, founded in 1932 by Fritz Kuhn to enroll Americans whose families had emigrated from Germany. Kuhn preached the usual Nazi message that Jews were organizing a conspiracy to impose communist governments worldwide. By 1939 he had about 20,000 followers – a tiny fraction of the millions of German-Americans.

Charles Coughlin (1891-1979) Pro-fascist broadcaster

Father Charles Coughlin was a Canadian-born Catholic priest who settled in Michigan and during the 1930s reached 40,000,000 listeners with his radio talks. His broadcasts became increasingly anti-Semitic and pro-fascist until 1942 when, with the USA at war with Nazi Germany, his superiors in the Church (at the request of the US government) finally shut him up.

Fascism's Frontiers

Europe in the early twentieth century had more influence in the world, through its colonies, trade and mass media, than it would after the Second World War. Aspects of fascism were sometimes attractive to new nations beyond Europe, in their struggle to define their identities, develop their economies or challenge the influence of Europe and the USA.

Latin America

Since achieving independence in the 1820s, most of the former colonies of Spain and Portugal had had a tradition of rule by the military or a 'strong man', at least for periods in their history. From the 1920s, Mussolini and then Hitler had admirers among the military in Latin America, and many ex-Nazis found refuge there after the Second World War. Many regimes in the region have been denounced as fascist for their violations of human rights (imprisonment without trial, torture of opponents, etc). However, in fact, these regimes more closely resemble Franco's

VENEZUELA
COLOMBIA
ECUADOR
PERU
BRAZIL
BOLIVIA
PARAGUAY
URUGUAY
ARGENTINA
CHILE
Falkland Is.

Chile

Unusually for Latin America, Chile achieved both prosperity and a stable democracy. But the 1929 world trade crisis threatened both. In 1932, Jorge Gonzalez von Marees, who was half Spanish and half German, founded a National Socialist Movement in Chile. Modelled on the German Nazis, it was supported by German migrants to Chile. It attempted an uprising in 1938 but this was easily suppressed by government troops. Gonzalez relaunched the movement as the Popular Socialist Vanguard but was imprisoned on suspicion of being mad and the Vanguard disbanded in 1941.

Brazil

Plinio Salgado visited Italy in 1930 and was deeply impressed by it. In 1932 he founded Brazilian Integralist Action. By 1934 it had 200,000 members, who wore green shirts – the colour of Brazil's flag. In his book *Let's Wake Up the Nation*, Salgado called on his followers to ignore party politicians as irrelevant and devote themselves to rousing the ordinary people, from whose unselfish work and sacrifices a new Brazil would be born. The movement was suppressed by Brazil's dictator, Getúlio Vargas, in 1937. Two Integralist revolts were crushed in 1938. After Salgado left for exile in Portugal in 1939, the movement fizzled out for lack of a leader.

Spain in their reliance on the support of the armed forces, the rich landowning class and, usually, the Church, especially against communists.

Argentina

In 1900, Argentina was one of the ten richest countries in the world. It attracted massive immigration, especially of Italians, who came to account for one third of the population. Not surprisingly, Argentina developed close ties with Mussolini's Italy.

In 1943, a 'Group of United Officers' seized power in Argentina. One of them, Juan Peron (1895-1974), had lived in Italy and visited Nazi Germany and Franco's Spain. He took control of the trade union movement and won the votes of its members to become president of Argentina in 1946. He then created a mass party to widen his support beyond the unions.

As '*El Lider*', Peron put businesses owned by US and British companies under Argentine state control and used the wealth built up from Argentina's wartime trade to raise wages. Aided by his film-star wife, Evita (1919-52), he attacked the power of rich landowners and funded schools and clinics for the poor *descamisados* ('shirtless'). Both Peron and Evita were brilliant public speakers and skilled at projecting an image of charm and concern. Both were also equally prepared to suppress critical newspapers and have opponents imprisoned and beaten up.

A crowd in Rugino, Santa Fe, greets Eva Peron and her husband, Juan, the president of Argentina.

Peronism without Peron

Re-elected president in 1951, Peron was weakened by the sudden death from cancer of the hugely popular Evita. Accusations of widespread corruption and Peron's own erratic decision-making led the army to force him into exile in Franco's Spain in 1955. Peronism, however, unlike Chilean Nacismo or Brazilian Integralism, survived the loss of its leader to remain a continuing force in Argentine politics.

Peron returned from exile in 1973 to be re-elected president and preside over mounting chaos. After his death the presidency passed to his ex-dancer third wife, Isabel (1931–), whom he had promoted as a second Evita. She proved far less competent than the real Evita and was exiled to Spain by the army in 1976. In 1989 Carlos Menem was elected president for the Peronist Justicialist Party, pledged to uphold democracy and return businesses from state to private control. This was the opposite of Peron's policies – but Menem still traded on the magic of his name.

" A middle way?

Like other populist dictators, Peron cultivated the image of himself as a super-hero blend of action man and deep thinker. He was indeed army fencing champion, a boxer and skier and had read widely in history and philosophy. Writing about what he called 'Justicialism' – a middle way between capitalism and communism – made him look serious-minded. But his own definition of Justicialism was just a list of contradictions: *'Christian and humanist with the best attributes of collectivism and individualism, idealism and materialism'*. In reality, Peron ignored theory in favour of practice, energetically doing whatever came to hand or seemed necessary to keep hold of power.

Japan

Japan resembled Germany. It was united after 1868 under an emperor and aristocratic leadership, and had a weak parliament and a strong bureaucracy. It had been swiftly industrialized, had a well-equipped army and navy, and was rapidly building an empire. Fighting alongside its ally, Britain, in the First World War, Japan was rewarded with former German possessions in the Pacific – the Caroline, Marshall and Marianas Islands.

In the 1920s, various challenges shook Japan's progress towards a prosperous Western-style democracy. The new League of Nations rejected Japan's proposal for a declaration of racial equality in its Charter. Japan wanted international recognition of the dignity of all 'civilized' peoples, whatever their colour. Other countries, such as Australia, took this as an indirect attack on their right to enforce a 'whites only' immigration policy. In 1924 the USA banned Japanese immigration. The Japanese took these insults as proof of Western racism towards Japan. In 1923, a huge earthquake caused colossal damage and killed 100,000 people in Tokyo and Yokohama. And Japan's

Japanese Empire, 1920s

population continued to grow at an alarming rate, causing poverty in rural areas.

Japanese politicians seemed weak and divided in the face of these problems. Small groups of extremists attracted junior army officers, students and intellectuals by attacking the power of big business and demanding help for Japanese farmers, stronger armed forces and a bigger empire overseas to settle surplus population. Although none of these groups grew into a mass movement, they did influence thinking in the army and among some politicians.

The world trade collapse of 1929–31 caused great hardship in Japan. In 1931, army commanders in Korea, a Japanese colony, invaded the neighbouring resource-rich Chinese province of Manchuria. This was done without the permission of the Japanese government, but the government then backed up the commanders rather than admit it had lost control. Japan was expelled from the League of Nations but hung on to Manchuria, making it a puppet state, Manchukuo. Japan then allied with Germany and Italy, which had also left the League.

In 1936, junior officers in Tokyo led an army revolt, killing several government ministers before being arrested by loyal troops. This event strengthened the position of army commanders, who said they could only control unruly juniors if the army and navy ministers (who were always serving officers, not politicians) had even more say in government policy. In 1937,

Nakano Seigo
The cost of speaking out

Journalist Nakano Seigo (1886-1943) was elected eight times to Japan's parliament, which he came to see as hopelessly corrupt. He met both Mussolini and Hitler and felt they were the type of heroic leader that Japan needed. Nakano formed a blackshirted Far East Society which attracted thousands but never became a real mass movement. He also attacked the Imperial Rule Assistance Association as incapable of rousing the people. As a result, the government forbade him to make speeches or publish articles and put him under house arrest, where he committed suicide by cutting out his stomach, samurai-style.

Japanese forces began a full-scale invasion of China, and in 1938, the Japanese government began to organize the country for all-out war, banning strikes and taking control of industry and the media. In 1940, the government, now dominated by the military, ordered all political parties to merge into an Imperial Rule Assistance Association, which had no power but meant that Japan still looked as though it had a parliament. In the same year Japanese forces advanced into Southeast Asia.

Japan's aggression brought war with Britain, the USA and their allies. Japan was allied with Germany and Italy, but made no effort to work with them and, in effect, fought its own, separate war. Eventually war brought defeat and occupation by the Allies, who enforced a new democratic constitution.

Was Japan fascist?

Japan certainly had fascist features in the decade before its defeat in 1945:

- strong anti-communism
- belief in its own racial superiority and historical traditions
- state control of industry for war
- state control of parliament, unions and media
- secret police and imprisonment of political opponents

But, as a non-European culture and society, it could have no trace of fascism's pro-Catholic, anti-Jewish elements. There was no mass party to stir up the population and take over existing institutions. There was no leader figure challenging the emperor. He remained a remote, largely powerless figurehead – but survived Japan's defeat to link the past with Japan's successful post-war transition to democracy.

South Africa

In 1815 Britain took over Cape Town and Natal on the coast of South Africa, and English-speaking settlers arrived to join the Dutch 'Afrikaners', who spoke Afrikaans. When Britain banned slavery, many Afrikaner Boers (farmers) made the Great Trek (1838) inland and founded the Transvaal and Orange Free State republics. After two wars to defend their independence, the Boers were forced to join their republics with Cape Town and Natal in the Union of South Africa. Many Boers remained bitterly anti-British and convinced of their racial superiority over South Africa's black majority, a belief supported by the teachings of the Afrikaners' Dutch Reformed Church. They formed a semi-secret society, the *Broederbond* (Brothers' Association) to uphold Afrikaner interests. In the 1930s, encouraged by Nazi Germany, German immigrants in South Africa formed an anti-Jewish Greyshirt paramilitary movement.

In 1938, Afrikaners re-enacted the Great Trek to mark its centenary. Out of this came a fascist movement, the *Ossewabrandwag* (OB, Ox-Wagon Guard), with a paramilitary wing, the *Stormjaers*. OB leaders, claiming 170,000 members, secretly offered Nazi agents an uprising in the event of war between Germany and Britain. The plan was that, after taking over government, the OB would grant the Nazis naval and air bases and take over southern Rhodesia (Zimbabwe) and other neighbouring countries. This plot was foiled by South African police in 1941.

Uniformed right-wing paramilitaries march through Pretoria, the South African capital. Note the swastika-like symbol on the flag.

From 1948 onwards, however, an Afrikaner-led National Party government began to enact apartheid laws, which protected the wealth and power of the white minority against South Africa's black, Asian and mixed-race population. When anti-apartheid struggles led to strikes, riots and campaigns of sabotage in the 1960s, the example of the OB influenced the founding of the *Afrikaner Werstandsbeweging* (AWB, African Resistance Movement) in 1973. Believing that apartheid did not go far enough in upholding white supremacy, the AWB aimed to found a separate 'independent Christian, republican Afrikaner-Boer state' to be rid of non-whites, Jews, communists, liberals, etc. The AWB's paramilitary, the Storm Falcons, and vigilantes, the *Brandwag*, have committed terrorist acts. The AWB denies being a fascist movement, describing itself as 'Christian-Nationalist'. As post-apartheid South Africa struggles towards inter-racial understanding, the AWB retains a measure of support in traditional Afrikaner rural strongholds.

Yesterday and Today

Despite the destruction of the major fascist states in the Second World War, thousands of organizations have been created to revive or reformulate fascist beliefs. They range from paramilitary terror groups to publishers and political parties. Conferences held in Rome, Italy, in 1950 and Malmo, Sweden, in 1951 launched the European Social Movement to unite fascists in 16 countries to fight for an anti-communist 'European Empire'. In 1962, a World Union of National Socialists was launched.

Some of these organizations try to launder the history of fascism, denying its crimes. Others try to restate fascism's aims in the post-war world: 'defending' Europe against the increased power of the USA, Russia or Asia or resisting the immigration of non-

Jean-Marie Le Pen
Paratrooper for president?

Le Pen (born 1928) is a former French paratrooper who, in 1972, united several squabbling factions into the *Front National*, with himself as president. He has campaigned strongly against the 2,000,000 Muslim Arab immigrants in France. Government officials and AIDS sufferers have also been targeted as public enemies. In 1986, 35 FN deputies were elected to parliament after securing 10 per cent of the vote to become France's fifth largest party. Le Pen polled 14 per cent in the election for president in 1988, 15 per cent in 1995 and 17 per cent in 2002.

Europeans. Others argue that the only way of tackling issues such as AIDS, drugs, street crime, pollution, urban decay and unemployment is for the young people who are the main victims of these problems to come together in fascist movements of national renewal based on self-sacrifice and teamwork.

Almost all neo-fascist groupings have been tiny, fringe bodies with little impact on the real world of politics. Willingness to use violence has sometimes given them publicity out of proportion to their numbers and helped them recruit among skinheads and soccer hooligans.

Fascist failure is no reason for democrats to be complacent. In Romania in 1993, a Party of the National Right was formed to campaign for the expulsion of all non-Romanians. In Russia, the 1993 general elections made Vladimir Zhirinovsky's misleadingly-named Liberal Democratic Party the third largest grouping in the Duma (parliament). Zhirinovsky has predicted that the USA will be

Violence erupts at a railway station near Copenhagen, Denmark, after a Neo-Nazi march marking the tenth anniversary of the death of German Nazi Rudolf Hess.

Vladimir Zhirinovsky at a demonstration in support of Yugoslavia, at the time of the crisis in Kosovo, October 1998.

broken up by conflict between its white and non-white citizens, and that a reborn Russia – purged of Ukrainians, Armenians, Baltic minorities, etc – will ally itself with a reborn Germany, including its 'lost' territories, to defend 'White Civilization'. The rest of Europe will be carved up to create an Arab state in southern France and turn Holland over to homosexuals. Zhirinovsky's vision is a world of 'less contact, no technical aid, no education of foreign specialists and students ... giving the opportunity for all races, nations and peoples to develop their civilizations IN PARALLEL, without mixing' – apartheid on a global scale. The emergence of this sort of visionary clap-trap in the chaos of post-communist Russia is yet another example of fascism as a political infection of societies in crisis.

Never Forget

Primo Levi (1919-87) was an Italian Jew and partisan who survived Auschwitz. He warned of the dangers of forgetting what fascism did:

'... what happened could happen again ... For this reason it is everyone's duty to reflect on what happened.

Everybody must know ... that when Hitler and Mussolini spoke in public, they were believed, applauded, admired, adored like gods ... The ideas they proclaimed ... were ... silly or cruel. And yet they were acclaimed ... and followed to the death by millions of the faithful.

We must remember that these faithful followers ... were ordinary men ... ready to believe and act without asking questions.

It is therefore necessary to be suspicious of those who seek to convince us with means other than reason ...

A new fascism ... can be born ... walking on tiptoe and calling itself by other names ... the memory of what happened in the heart of Europe, not very long ago, can serve as a warning ...'

Despairing that post-war generations had forgotten the horrors of fascism or, worse still, believed historical lies that fascist atrocities had never happened, Levi committed suicide in 1987.

DATE LIST

1871	Unification of Germany. Unification of Italy.
1883	Birth of Benito Mussolini.
1889	Birth of Adolf Hitler.
1914–18	First World War.
1917	Revolution in Russia.
1919	Versailles Treaty ends the First World War. D'Annunzio seizes Fiume. Mussolini founds first fascist squad. Hitler joins German Workers' Party.
1920	Admiral Horthy becomes Regent of Hungary.
1921	Mussolini founds the National Fascist Party.
1922	Fascist March on Rome.
1923	Hitler founds the SA and the SS. Failed Nazi uprising in Munich. General Primo de Rivera becomes dictator of Spain.
1924	Fascists murder Giacomo Matteotti.
1925	Hitler publishes *Mein Kampf*. Mussolini becomes *Il Duce*.
1926	Fascist party becomes the only legal party in Italy. General Carmona seizes power in Portugal.
1927	Corneliu Codreanu founds the Legion of the Archangel Michael in Romania.
1929–31	Collapse of world trade causes mass unemployment.
1929	Mussolini negotiates Lateran Accords. Anti-communist Lapua movement emerges in Finland. Estonian War of Independence League founded.
1930	Codreanu forms the Iron Guard.
1931	Japanese forces invade Manchuria.
1932	Sir Oswald Mosley founds the British Union of Fascists. Friends of the New Germany founded in the USA. Army Comrades Association founded in Ireland. Nationalist Socialist movement founded in Chile. Brazilian Integralist Action founded.
1933	Hitler becomes Chancellor of Germany. Salazar introduces the *Estado Novo* in Portugal. José Antonio Primo de Rivera founds the Falange in Spain. Vidkun Quisling founds the National Union in Norway.
1934	Hitler becomes *Führer*. Salazar dissolves National Syndicalists. Karlis Ulmanis becomes dictator of Latvia.
1935–36	Italian conquest of Ethiopia.
1935	Nazi 'Nuremberg Laws' deprive German Jews of basic civil rights. Ferenc Szalasi founds the Party of National Will in Hungary.
1936–39	Spanish Civil War.
1936	German troops reoccupy the Rhineland. Olympic Games held in Berlin. British Union of Fascists routed in the 'Battle of Cable Street'. Leon Degrelle founds the Rex party in Belgium. Junior officers revolt in Japan.
1937	Franco makes the Falange Spain's only political party. Japan invades China.

1938	Austria becomes part of Germany. Great Trek centenary leads to founding of the Ox-Wagon Guard in South Africa.
1939–45	Second World War.
1939	Germany takes over German-inhabited Sudetenland region of Czechoslovakia. Slovakia becomes independent.
1940	General Antonescu becomes *Conducator* of Romania. British fascists imprisoned. Pro-Nazi government established in France. Imperial Rule Assistance Association founded in Japan.
1941	Japan attacks US base at Pearl Harbor. Germany invades the USSR and declares war on USA. Croatia becomes independent. Antonescu crushes Iron Guard.
1943	Collapse of fascism in Italy. Mussolini founds the Italian Social Republic. Group of United Officers seizes power in Argentina.
1944	Slovak army revolt.
1945	Hitler commits suicide. Mussolini is killed by partisans. Quisling is executed.

1946	Antonescu and Szalasi executed. Juan Peron elected President of Argentina.
1951	European Social Movement founded. Italian Social Movement founded.
1952	Death of Eva Peron.
1962	World Union of National Socialists founded.
1968	Salazar resigns from power in Portugal.
1973	Peron returns from exile to become president of Argentina. African Resistance Movement founded in South Africa.
1975	Franco dies. Spain becomes a democracy under King Juan Carlos I.
1976	Democracy established in Portugal.
1993	Party of the National Right formed in Romania.
2002	Local elections see the British National Party gain 3 council seats in Burnley - its first gains for nine years.

GLOSSARY

anti-Semitism
hatred of Jews.

autonomy
control over one's own affairs.

Aryan
member of the highest racial group in the Nazi pyramid of human types. The word originally described a group of languages spoken in northern India, from which both German and English have developed. Later the word meant people who spoke those languages. They were thought of as an ancient race of tough warriors of great beauty and high intelligence. The language link is a matter of history. The idea of a heroic 'master race' has no basis.

censorship
control of information to support a particular point of view.

civil war
war between different groups within one country about how it should be governed.

coalition
an alliance of political parties or groups, usually to form or oppose a government.

communism
government based on the idea that a single ruling political party can run a country for all its people's benefit better than if they are left to make their own decisions and keep their own private homes, land and businesses. In practice, communist governments have usually been cruel dictatorships.

democracy
system of government based on the equal rights of all citizens to speak on political matters and take part freely in choosing their leaders.

dictatorship
government by a ruler with complete power, not answerable to a parliament.

land reform
dividing large estates into smaller farms to share out land more fairly.

League of Nations
international organization founded in 1920 to encourage cooperation and peaceful settlement of conflicts between nations; it was succeeded by the United Nations in 1946.

left-wing
favouring socialism or radical social reform.

Liberal
favouring individual rights, moderate social reform and freedom from close government control.

Mafia
secret criminal organization based in Sicily and southern Italy.

militia
amateur armed force, usually uniformed and trained part-time, normally for use only in emergencies.

national socialist
follower of the Nazi party.

nativism
belief in the superiority of the traditions of one's own country and people.

neo-fascist
follower of a movement founded in imitation of the Fascists.

neo-Nazi
follower of a movement modelled on the Nazis.

paramilitary
group organized on military lines, often uniformed and armed, to support a political grouping.

RESOURCES

partisan
guerrilla fighter against invaders or army of occupation.

patriotic
devoted to one's country.

propaganda
methods of publicity and persuasion using symbols and slogans to gain support for or against a cause, group, party or person.

rally
political mass meeting, often arranged to stir up emotion by means of shouting slogans, beating drums, waving flags, marching in processions.

reparations
payments intended to make up for damage caused by war.

republic
system of government headed by an elected president rather than a king or emperor born to be a ruler.

right-wing
favouring traditional institutions.

secret police
police force, often working outside the law, used to control political opponents of a government.

socialist
person who believes that a country's wealth should be shared out more equally. Unlike communists, socialists accept democracy and changes of government by free elections.

trade unions
organizations to defend and extend the rights and living standards of working people, usually based on a particular (group of) occupation(s).

Novels
Fatherland (Arrow, 1993), by Robert Harris, is a thriller set in a Nazi-run Europe, 20 years after the Nazis have won the Second World War.

Italian novelist Giorgio Bassani drew on his life among the Jewish community in Ferrara to write *The Garden of the Finzi-Continis* (Cabaret, 1972), which describes how a wealthy Jewish family is wiped out by the Nazis.

Films
Cabaret (1972), set in 1930s Berlin, describes the rise of Nazism, showing how many people failed to take it seriously until too late. The film is loosely based on Christopher Isherwood's 1935 novel, *Mr Norris Changes Trains*, which drew on Isherwood's experiences as an English teacher in Berlin at that time.

Steven Spielberg's *Schindler's List* (1993) is sometimes wilfully inaccurate in its details, but conveys a horrifying sense of conditions in a Nazi death-camp.

Alan Parker's 1996 film version of the Tim Rice/Andrew Lloyd Webber musical *Evita* gives a brilliant impression of the crowd-pleasing style of the Peronist movement.

Sir Ian McKellen's film version of Shakespeare's *Richard III* (1996) presents the villainous king as a 1930s-type fascist dictator, complete with Nazi-style uniforms.

The prize-winning Italian film *La Vita e Bella* (*Life is Beautiful*, 1999) shows how an Italian Jewish father uses humour to disguise from his little son the horror of the death awaiting them at the hands of the Nazis.

INDEX